HOOTING ACROSS THE SILENCE

HOOTING

Horizon Press   New York

ACROSS THE SILENCE

Poems by HY SOBILOFF

To Margaret

It is hard to believe that this is Hy Sobiloff's last book of poems. A busy man—and a businessman active as ten—he never stopped writing poems. *Hooting Across the Silence* is his fifth book, but he had enough to fill fifty. He winnowed, he rewrote, he discarded armloads of poems—others he would speak aloud and never write down. In his splashing fountain of poems with its perpetual lifting energy and flow filtered through by masses of light and passing shadow, there is always underlying, where it counts most for the true shape of feeling in them, an astonishing stammer, the stammer of honesty.

This is what gets to us and also keeps the poems from looking "finished." Yet all are there in their essential ineradicable being, not unfinished but crouching and waiting to back up against the poem before, or to prompt the next one, like "Walls taking sides against each other." Walls or field forces of walls, they move on, having to register what is seen, including the "fingerprints of recollections," and take account of all presence while on the run: "As I shrug my common sense/Hide behind my own two eyes/Then run to the end of sight."

Running? Running where? (*Running* sounds as though they have no place to go.) Towards joy, I'd say. This is the most recurrent word, and this is where all of Hy's subjects aim, or where in spite of their subjects his poems, like quick drawn bows, strain toward: "How deep the rolling/Elongated curved caterpillar trailers'/Plump bellies, bursting with Nature's fruit!" are the open-

3

ing lines of his sequence, *The West St. Market*. And the joy sur-
charging such words is not different from the feeling in a poem
about the plight of a passenger, embraced in the macabre, con-
centration-camp reference, "She totters upon an auschwitz cross-
town/Bus, morgue-faced . . ." Can the lady be going to join, or is
she related to, the monstrous, self-satisfied ladies in the next one,
Three Chapeaux Having Lunch?

> *Plump hands, with spoons, sipped up the soup,*
> *Pressed napkins to their chirping lips.*
> *They looked the way they thought they ought*
> *To look in case you looked or cared*
> *For feathers and quills, leather and fur.*

Hy Sobiloff, who could write so well about how it feels to be
acutely alive in mid-century New York, knew voracious women
(Blind Date and *Man Eater)*, warmed to his dead friends *(Losses)*
and parents *(Reunion* and *Aspects of Papa)* and, under a dock at
dawn *(Before the Sail)*, while waiting for the men to start their
boats, had a vision glowing with a lonely joy:

> *A stuttering outboard started up, stopped, started,*
> *Choked on an echo . . .*
>
> *An hour more, then life would begin,*
> *The noisy, the bargaining affection.*

But the final word to start the cycle of reading him again, flying
down from an upside-down sky, is in *Surprise*, maybe his own best
epitaph:

4

I climbed my limbs into wings.
One shallow wing fell down
And down I fell. What could I think
Up in the sky? What does a bird

Think? Weird, crippled sky-flier!
Bird-man with one gimpy wing!
The earth, falling, amazes me
As I rise to meet the ground.

Yes, it's only the earth that's falling, Hy Sobiloff, while you go on flying in the joys and surprises of your poems.

—Edwin Honig

Invocation

Grateful, uncovered sounds brush on the grass
Fireflies, lighting up, bite at the night
Dog packs of stars rehearse their howls
Stairs to look up to, wind-chimes
Among soft cusps and thin collisions.

Contents

HOOTING ACROSS THE SILENCE

Abandonment

Sly metamorphoses along the route
Flicker in shrouds, beckon from vacant lots
And downhill caves, recalling broken promises:
Remember me? Remember me! Remember me!

With all my ponderous pledges of faith,
My accustomed ideals, acid-cursed,
My philosophical goods and truths, etc.,
And all the rest of the spirit's baggage,
I kneel on the yoke of an aimless trapeze
Whipped by lariat shadows, star-pierced, and rise
Into vacancy, my feet sinking in words.

Memory walks from episode to episode
Ringing the bells of self-evicted residences.
I make discreet inquiries, "Where do I live?"

Carpe Diem

Depending on luck,
The swift or lingering end,
Continually packing and unpacking for disaster,
I am too much aware of being and unbeing.

How can I manage amazement,
Enjoy and recognize joy,
Shed my fear of losing, betraying
The up-bursting moment of time
I'm alive in, full of her hope?

My mind's confined to where I am,
A letter box, deeper than I think,
In which to drop remembrances,
Thank You notes, tearful anniversaries,
The fingerprints of recollections.

Up the Ladder

The legendary witch, outlasting joy,
Once taught me to jam fear down my throat,
To wash the holy madness out of dreams,
To practice smiles, shake hands, fists,
Kick a can across a field and munch
Half-ripe grapes on the edge of my teeth.

Bolted in closets, doomed for my own good,
Forbidden to scream out in anger,
I settled at last into a strange station,
Muffling laughter in funereal shades.
But the blind learn to read in blindness,
The mute flutter, touch, gasp communication.

Inventory

Paused in the middle
Of my small life,
A temporary place,
I lounge in my remains.

An old man in a trunk
Like a Jack-in-the-box
Pops into my thoughts—
But I keep the lid shut.

I neither make up dreams
Nor unriddle oracles:
I am a musician who wheezes
Do re me fa so up on tiptoe.

Those years are now a drowse
Of shadows, loveless myths,
When, in unkind inconstancies,
I tilted in other arms.

Yet I thought I might rock
Forever in childhood's ark,
Until my own damned circle
Tightened its diurnal whirlpool.

Crypt

Cold parsley of a high wet day
Brought to my taste
The honeycomb that glue-saps memory:

A hut in the forest where three bears lived;
The Quaker friend who cupped up incoherence;
The buzzing embarrassment of origins;
The bare comb that harrows my baldness.

Under My Skin

Baking home-style anxiety pies,
Cross-bordered, out-territoried,
Walked on, swum in, flown over
In the shrunk and wizened circle
Of freedom's tightening vise,
Startled, I saw stars on earth
Twinkle with wan-worn wisdom
And burst into constellations
Of laughter, shaking the apples
Of consequence and circumstance,
Overthrown stars, ripened and fabulous
Meteors caught with my own eyes!
An excuse to get out of the house.

Since I Last Saw You

I've been staying alive,
Drifting on driftwood

Through galactic spaces,
Following the gleam.

The first time I flew
I already knew how

Because, as a child,
I hawk-eyed the gosling,

Screamed a loud chirp
To ungrateful earth,

Then spread and swooped
Off on a revery.

Quiddity

All human particulars
And instancies of feeling
Are tied together by
Marks that identify.

The nightmare of a laugh
In my orderly dark room can
Slow down all reassurances and
Shams of dignity.

Weather-beaten by design,
Antiqued by nature,
I submit to all things
And compose my silences.

Is It Like

Indecisions in a maze
   Coming and going years colliding
Walls taking sides against each other
   Keys agitated in locks
   Dooms of waiting for bells
   Guilt beads that burst my pores
As I shrug my common sense
   Hide behind my own two eyes
   Then run to the end of sight.

Ecce Homo

Undressing the heavy load of self-loathing
From my hunched-up back of self,
I ran dry-mouthed from city mobs,
Baa-baa vigilantes, prophets of fear,
To lap from a trickle of hope.

My autumn time began to expire,
The vague future drifted to snow.
Lost was my infatuation for
Peddling my service through all seasons.
I crossed my limits and shrank
From the world I helped make weep;
Lived four deaths beyond my time,
Died, and was reborn every birthday;
Confounded threnody and lullaby
With the blurred, sand-blowing winds
That will erase my epitaph.

Interior

I let the world in through a switch
But coop my tongue inside its vault,
Practice privacy within my skull
And gargle away bad thoughts.

Squeezing the pent-up compliancies
Of fifty years with gibbets and frauds,
I press time's waste into a jar,
Sniff, remember, and flush down the shame.

A Faraway Eye

Childhood, my superstitious teacher,
Warned me the black crow longs for my carcass.
I would run from closet ghosts
Of black crows clutching my hair,
Confusing them with hats harassing me.
Something within me drew me here
To the haunts
Of the sleek black arrow bird,
Thrilled by fear, waiting for darkness,
Pulling feathers from a bare scalp
Until I heard the crow crow crow sounds.

Guide to the Perplexed

Heavy-laden, soaked with thought, the mind's
A raggedy mop that washes away footprints.
Start the singing from alcove or altar!
Follow the trail of sound, dance,
Awaken the slumberers,
Quake the room with important noises,
Annihilate distance with one embrace!

First Day of Spring
(For Norman Elson)

There was no sadness on that faunlike afternoon.
Erasing the numbers and headlines from my mind
I drove in a clopping hansom through the park
While the grinding mechanical World Wheel stopped.
No one was minding the store. The lazed fiesta
Spread out on lawns, faint hurdy-gurdy shrills
Piped through the air, junkman, banker and poet
Lay under one blue, sprawled upon one green.

Dawdlers and wanderers through the paths
All seemed at first to blend, merging
Into a vague unfocus of the same face;
Then, turning back twice, I saw their shapes
And singular expressions become their own.
At the edge of a fountain, quiet ones sat
Buttock to buttock in a narrow squeeze,
Lifeless as statuary, migrated from the park's
Peripheries to dwell within the inmost dazzle,
Padrones of lakes and zoos and carousels
A topple of blocks from walk-up tenements.
A shirtless man, shiftless in the sun,
Lay reddening, abandoned to a muse—
One self-willed fist kept tearing at the grass.
From a quickening distance I lip-read the mouths
Of mothers murmuring joy without words.

28

Two banjo blueprints, long-haired yodelers,
Strummed and twinned their high-up gladness.
Shy voyeurs, flinching, lowered their eyes
To scan the miniskirts that whipped on by.
Escaped hilarious ballons flew to the sun
Trailing their strings and children's tears behind.

What Time Is It?

Joy at night
When the city's stoplights click in silence
When the dentists stop drilling through the sidewalks
When I run from my bed to hear the hurdy-gurdy
Loins of music ring out of distances
Joy when my toys come strutting into the light.

So I sing in myself
Outharmonizing the rag-picking banker's wail
Burying the day's martyrdom of garbage and papers
And sip new wine at my own fiesta.
My words bounce like rain upon the trellises
As I thunder in my soliloquies.

I eat an enormous rooster,
My stomach swells and smiles
And I crow for my friends till it hurts
While we waltz out the night every night.

Witches' Coven

My cur and I trotted into a blind side alley
At midnight time, his call having arrived.
The city swarms had abandoned the streets—
Buses, trains, cars snored in their sleep stalls.
My cur and I together were the multitudes
Adrift in our own selves inside that alley.
I gazed at a scrap of venturous sky
Here where noise was beheaded and blank,
And a quiet spirit dawned within me
While the cur was rapt in his own business.

Clang-bang falsetto six-pack shameless screams
Jangled at once in quadrilateral alley echoes!
The concealed night lit up to banqueting cats!
Kicking the lids off garbage-can love nests,
They spring across darkness, these flying cats,
In spider shapes that scuttle through my mind.

The West St. Market

I

While the City Sleeps

How deep the rolling
Elongated curved caterpillar trailers'
Plump bellies, bursting with Nature's fruits!
All night the airbrakes
Hiss, exhausted, into this market
Where night-eyed sunless men
Compute and divide the spoils
Long before breakfast's on the table.

II

Truck Handler

Squat on a restaurant stool
He ate a doughnut slurped in coffee.
His hair fell over the cup,
The doughnut sugared his eyebrows,
Yet he sipped, swallowed and gulped
With his lips glued to the rim,
And his elbows guarded the spread
With the grapple of an old
Lion ready to spring.

III

Scavenger

Somebody's mother
Hops from truck to truck
To pick up the spillings
In an express-moving
Shrill-shouting fruit market.

Men look away
As she stoops, unembarrassed,
This shawled old screech owl,
To fill her vagrant hunger bag
With flayed tomatoes
Lopsided apples
Orphaned grapes
Witch-nosed carrots
For a day's deferment.

IV

The Forgotten

They meet around
A bouquet of fire
Struck in a barrel,
Their deep-hollowed,
Life-corroded faces
Glaring in flames.

On splintery crates
Some nod, shut-eyed,
Covered by sheets
Of yesterday's paper.
Lost words and snores
Steam from their mouths.

Under Repair

Near the traffic-honking corner
Of a torn-up, wood-planked street,
Caught in the city's maelstrom,
I stood bunched at the light-changer
With small confidence, my head
Sloped away from a rejected star.
Pedestrians, clutching, jammed the curb,
Constantly at the point of departure;
Girls in a tug-of-war with dogs
(Crazed forepaws scratching granite)
Strained, taut-leased, for a charge;
Beeping automobiles through open
Arteries bled into Central Park;
Speed-slowed to capacity, dizzy
Buses rode cross-town in circles;
Above me riveting steeplejacks
Were remaking hovering views . . . .

With a balled white handkerchief
I wiped the noises from my brow,
Waiting for the city to mend.
Nearby, a burbling fountain
Splashed a scarce mouthful,
Sadly washing the air.

Practical Joke

The traffic arrows
thrust
    without point
                dn
to the sky.
Down in
      the low—
            life region
(one block askew
  from the park and the green)
trafficwormsthrough
holes in misguided streets:
honking and friendless machines aw-
ry and bunched in their own gas.

What's New?

Wearing a full-blooded
Wine-redded clown's nose,
This tottering derelict
Snipes the New York *Times*
Out of a corner basket.
Life-estranged, his eyes
Refocus the headlines,
Skimp the obituaries,
Scowl over editorials
Like a swaying straphanger
With standing room only
In his own tight skin.
Done, he shuffles off
Garbled with events,
Muttering spitfire curses,
Uncorking a nip of venom.

Along the Boardwalk

Man and boy, sightless,
Upon rhythm-wracked planks
Sway in a wheelchair.

Blank stares tick and gaze,
Trance-carved mouths smile,
Frown, smile for unseen eyes.

Tips finger smooth parchment,
Caress and then drum the mind's
Insatiable calypso beat.

Hot Dog Man

Featherless biped
   Perched on a curbstone
      Smileless, in hurting weather,
Dancing in one spot to a numb rhythm of toes
   Rapping a tune with his tongs while rain
      Soaks through his faded striped umbrella:
Queer city bird, bird of all seasons,
   Stabbing up franks, clicking off change,
      Mumbling in half a silence, busily innocent,
His claw-cold hands repeat, repeat, repeat
And spread the mustard deftly on the bread
With or without chopped onion or sauerkraut.

On a Park Bench

An old woman knitting
Drops a stitch
Loses a niche
In her dream,
Falls back,
Picks, plucks,
Her intricate fingers
Willing a yarn of time,
Connecting thought to thought,
A bye-bye cradle rocking.

Getting Off, Please

Crushed standing up
On high heels, squeezed by her parcels,
She totters upon an Auschwitz crosstown
Bus, morgue-faced, while the driver
Seethes in the fuming traffic.

So then, like a schoolboy Blue Boy
Golden Rule boy out to please his Whistler's Mother,
Rising, I offer half a cheek of seat.
My minuet of courtesy
(Performed to absent raptures of applause)
Turned on a half-smile grudged across the aisle.

Three Chapeaux Having Lunch

A Porcupine, a Beaver, and a Felt
Sat together in a cozy nook
Chewing the chase and breaking words at brunch.
Plump hands, with spoons, sipped up the soup,
Pressed napkins to their chirping lips.
They looked the way they thought they ought
To look in case you looked or cared
For feathers and quills, leather and fur.

Circumstance

Being taught to begin again, a blind
Young girl with gawky steps stepped on my shadow.
It must have been her first blind street lesson.
Her metal tapper, testing the pavement,
Tapped out an arc, paused, tapped out another.
Her teacher, close beside her, groomed each step.
Just as they reached the curb, her sweetness rose—
The spring that was in her eyes—and, as a girl does,
She tucked her arm in his and skipped across.

Montauk Sit-Up

Back again from the temporary city,
I took with me all the permanence I breathed—
Unkillable portraits, sounds of portraits,
Hope, deep-rooted light, and no
Particular language of thought.
Under an elm tree I reconciled
The fall to leaves of absence,
Peered through a telescopic lens,
Welcomed the tender pips of buds.
Winter's noisy five months or so,
Tired of their own ugliness,
Thawed in shiftiness, lifted their scowls;
Colloidal nourishment began to squeeze
Its beauty through dark bark.
I walked beside the forehead of an ocean
Surrendering cracked frozen ripples.
Floating ducks in raindrops splashed
Between nightfuls of moon and crashes
Of daybreak, bird-chirp awakened.

Age of Aquarius

Two big-town con men, all of eight, hustled
A balding, middle-bulging, muddle-aging mark,
Myself, alas! at the corner of 69th and Lex:

"Hey, Mister, wanna see the moon for a nickel?"
My mind wept back, back, undressed my memory
To a summer roadside fifty hot summers ago:

Could it be *me* there selling 5¢ homemade lemonade? . . .
"If you don't see it, you can keep your nickel!"
That cinched the deal, that sold me the moon,

So I turned around the corner of time with them.
Against the curb, perched on a wobbly tripod,
Their telescope stood pointing up at the moon.

I almost swooned to see it swim into my ken,
The same old good old moon, as round, as full,
But dimmer than a brand-new buffalo nickel.

Prima Ballerina

My cockroach dances
To a kitchen feast,
Twists and goes,
A never bending
Nimbly twirling
Lady to her toes,
Tangos to the sink,
Waltzes to crumbs,
Flips to sour cream:
Prowler of pantries,
My pampered nightowl,
She wakes up only
When I fall asleep
To spend the dawn,
Then disappears
Into the word-work.

Credo

A girl (if a girl) 's a girl in a dress
That she puts on for us to size
Her up, admire her furbelows,
Take down her numbers and propose
The wine, the line, the pass, the pome!
Whether she flaunts her hair wind-blown
Or curled, whether she sprays Chanel
Or scrubs with soap, she wafts perfume
Whene're she struts on air or heels.
But when a girl (if a girl) wears pants
Her lovely ass stares out like an elephant's.

Tabby Tale

No one ever stops to ask a cat
Who the hell his father is.
Pedigreed in the darkness of pleasure,
Tabby now walks in anonymity.
Suave, elusive, shadow-stretched
And etched by headlights on macadam,
He disappears into a screech
To consummate his odyssey,
Then slinks back, whisker-bent,
Tail-tuckered to Penelope.

Love's Jaw Bone

The statue in the back yard now stands bare
As a desert jaw bone, a freak of love,
Her marble fingers frozen by her side.

Raw seasons uncovered
Her head bent shy
And white, tilted in a frame
Awaiting spring's halo.

Pictures at an Exhibition

Hung single-file a thousand years apart
Through bare-webbed narrowing corridors
They jostle and collide, glaring their eyes
In sibling rivalries and tribal feuds,
Arraigned before a waddling flock of necks,
Busy-body collectors and connoisseurs,
Cricket-tickers computing and swapping
Popularities and pedigrees and signatures,
The babel and din of critical auctioneers
Muting their spirits, fazing their cries,
Snuffing the live wick of Aladdin's lamp.

Playground

I

Higher and Higher

Instinctive, ever moving,
Children with pent-up legs
Screech on seesaws
Slide down, climb up rungs
Share swift perils
Bruised by knees
Dried by tears
Scaredest memory
Played out, forgot
Whooping once more—
Light of all living
To sit rocking their
Echoes, shouting
Shouts of joy in
Pure notes of feeling.

II

War

Johnny Brooks banged his brother Sam,
Banged him with a biff and a bam;
Sam waded in with his vorpal sword
And a kiss from Mom was his reward.
Umpah, Mama! Umpah, Papa!
Hah! Hah! Hah! Hah!

III

Here He Is

I found a lost child—
A cold and unfed sleepyhead
Snuggled under a tree—
Then whistled three conversations
Awakened him with a timothy feather
Lifted him from his warm new bed—
He washed his eyes with a look at me.
I told him cuckoobird stories
Then together we chug-chugged home.

Draw Me a Cow

Cows love earth
With their teeth
Graze up, down
A moo meadow
Flip their tails
Swat flies
Twist on grassbeds
Sleep on four legs
Their tongues snore
In an open mouth.

Proto

Let me return to before
Float back to trees
Hang, swing, climb
Curve my hands
Flutter birds
Grunt laughter
Thump my chest
Feel hair grow
Flatter myself
Behave like man.

Fame

Is that me with sword in hand?
Am I already cast in bronze
And stumped in a city park?
What plaque or bust am I
Beaten by all the seasons?
What age eclipses infancy?
The stretch from one to ninety
Is a loving sculptured mound
Pigeoned upon, rained upon,
Smoothed by children's fingers.
Will they pat my prowlike profile?
Will they rubadub my dates?

Exodus

What's the earth for?
Ten million citizens hanging in air,
Window-blinded by wishes,
Chute down shafts to the ground
From mountainous rookeries
Chopped into cubicles
To find plumage for the mind,
Style for the bottom,
Pudding for the belly.

Carbon-choked, exhaust-blurred,
Crushed by thunderous prisms,
On streets empty of songbirds
They flock among punctual vultures
Who feast on carrion of dead time.

Under the Greenwood Tree

It was a dew-fresh summer sunrinse dawn.
My restlessness and careless joy
Mingling with bird sounds,
Barefoot I ran to join their early choruses.

Wafting my eyes high up
From branch to branch of fluttering notes,
Magic opened my mouth:
I whistled, they whistled, taut-throated
We whistled together questions and answers,
Antiphonal kyries, kyries and hallelujahs,
As though a spirit conducted the dawn.

Pledge of Allegiance

Mother Nature's loyal subject,
Neither perplexed nor alarmed by her dead calms or rage,
I let the rain fall on me
Or sit inside and watch it swell through the gutter,
Washing and puddling the streets.
Sometimes I beg my Mother
For a peek of sun;
Sometimes for snow to roll in, ski on,
To raise the smudged eye up to a white hill
Where children bellywhop down and shout
And icicles melt from their breath.

I too fear her
Whenever she kills a tree
Or sends one small flood to sink the land like a ship.
She forms ice-caps over deserts,
Tears off moons, explodes planets, unravels galaxies.

But then she forgives and grows flowers back,
Animals back, people back.
Because I love her, I know it is not through my window
Her lightning strikes.

Nuclear

perennial soil
yields phosphorescent
volcanic flowers
and scepters of rosebuds

white water lilies
and red dragon plants
hide under a mirror's
crystalline surface

original granite
thaws in springtime's
out-of-the-world flights
and storms of reason

The Hummingbird Caper

Hummingbird, bird whose wings cross seas,
Hum and hover over my swimming pool!

Once you stood still in mid-air
Atremble in the library,
A tiny-muscled bee of a bird
Whose tail quickens with balance.

I could not find you at first
But heard your frenzy:
With a broom, bird's throne, I tried
Again and again to launch your breath.

Why did you fly back
Stubbornly to the window,
Trapped by sight,
And peck and peck at the glass?

Your strong sharp tiny beak
That could cut through hurricane winds
Was mocked and thwarted
Until at last I set you free.

In clear, familiar air
Your headstrong humming
Proclaims an inch of God's imagination
Whose compass zooms the world.

Fertilizing Brook-Fern

Narrow, unseen,
Yet seen through me
(A hooded photographer
Peering into his sights)
My fingers fidgeted
To spread the view:

Breeding, wriggling
In winter's morning,
Warmed by rugged covers,
An unworlded meeting
Of wildest beauty—
Parallel to a brook
Fern fields fanned out.

Spring's elfland bells
Chimed back phenomena
Of banished sprites,
Curled embryonic sprouts:
Winter's ends swelling,
Brook thaws gushing
In a maculate wasteland.

Where Fingers Make a Face

Huddled together on a lake walk
With half-frozen ideas, moonlight shadowed,
The cold pinch of winter apples our cheeks,
Snow petals hiss on subterranean pyres
Where widowed lawns still burn through frost,
We fleece with our eyes the sheep's-wool valleys,
Pluck off and taste white-icicled pine needles
(The hot frostbite tingles on the tongue)
Then ski down muscled slopes and fly again.

Wild Life

Right in the middle of the lawn, *look!* it's a rabbit
Set there as solid as a buddha, stone-still and sun-striped
By nervous tree-branch camouflage. Down on knees,
Holding on to bunch knaps, compressing my breath,
I stalked slow motion, slow as a gnomon,
And reached within three whiskery blades of grass . . .
Perked up, aware, sniffling,
The bell of instinct rang, it turned to flesh,
Twitch-tailed about and rapidly kangarooed away.

Years ago I practiced noiselessness, how to play dead
Belly-flat on the grass, but even the slowest birds
Discovered my breathing, and the rabbits, the rabbits
(Having learned to survive snake fangs, cat claws,
Stiletto-toothed foxes and man's steel traps and guns)
Stayed in their safety zones three blades away.
Rabbits are natural friends who aren't so friendly—
They know us too well.
                    And yet, somehow, I always longed
To fence one in with carrots to munch, milk to lap.
The ancient boy in me (not the savage) stood up and shouted:
"Come back, rabbit! Don't be scared! I won't eat you!"

De Gustibus

Coming or going,
I never liked railroad stations;
Likewise, they cold-stare at me
As if I were excess freight or disposal baggage.
Sometimes, puffing in ahead of time,
Uneasiness would wet under my arms
And I'd run, slowly, under the shade of a big clock—
All railroad stations surround a big clock—
So that I'd almost miss the train hiding under that clock,
But a racking squawk-box sounds off:
"*Bjaughrrkmmnopique . . . !*"

On the other hand, I like piers and docks—
The seaweed-braiding water is my friend.
I can sit and dangle at the end of a dock
At the edge of my mind, reeling in fantasies.
I put my ear to the planks to hear boat-dock talk-talk.
There's always someone likeable,
someone with time on his hands,
To chew up scores or memories.
Even the brine-corroded nails are friendly.

I once sat around a fellow cleaning his catch.
His steady, articulated knife scaled and gutted
Each fish with an artist's brush stroke.
Without my asking, he handed me a six-pounder,
Threw the gizzards to cats and shuffled on,
Letting the fish hawks fend for themselves.
Piers and docks—also the people on piers and docks—
They have a modest friendliness, an openness,
Almost like a loving woman's
Open and outstretched arms.

Shells

Driven from the sea by scouring tides
How prettily they lie
Stretched out in rows across my shelf!
I give each shell a name

And feelings to replace its emptiness.
Poor shell, so dispossessed
From the wild, remorseless, mindless sea
That I came to pick up

By chance along a windy stretch of sand,
Queer fragment of a coral
Dynasty now banished and uncoiled and flung
Through thought-spinning years.

Sentimental Fallacy

This dawn-skimming bird
Re-echoes my scream
Rinses its wings
Preens its feathers
In foamy shallows.

It keeps its distance
Wary of the shore
But swoops and carouses
Like a sailor on a spree
With each change of tide.

Out of the Blue

Like a floating island
I don't know why I swam away . . .

With courage not yet stronger than desire
I learned to walk in shallow coral waters,
My wrinkled soles cross-hatched by wounds;
But each day, hardened, I bled less and less.
Poking at low tide, squeeze-toed in the muck,
My head swung, lantern-eyed, this way, that way,
Peering through greenish-brown to scar-black
Seaweed layers that mummify the gaping shells.
On my knees now, digging through sand sockets
To spear sly limpets trap-doored in their castles,
I watched their squirms emerge like silent screams,
Then held one up, stuck on my lance, sun-gilt,
Struck blind by miles of faceted and sparkling
Sand grains ground into diamonds by the sea.

Sand Castle

Children's quick eyes
   Scoop up the shore
Imagination fills their hands
   With sea-weeds
     Married to ear-shells
They race beyond a father's voice
To where each stone's a friend
   A jigsaw joy
     In an unfastened day—
One glance overflows their eyes
Yet the seascape includes them gladly.

Before the Sail

Pacing about alone
On the deck of a morning dressed in sunshine,
I squinted and scanned
The shimmering, trancelike harbor:
A sailboat, tied to a pole,
Bobbed quietly, awaiting
The breeze of freedom;
Hungover yachts, abandoned
Dormitories, lay listless, crewless;
Gulls shrieked and tested
Sea and foam hunger;
A stuttering outboard started up, stopped, started,
Choked on an echo . . .

An hour more, then life would begin,
The noisy, the bargaining affection.

Rare Encounter

On a bobbing teakwood deck, an ant,
An ant at play,
An ant without a hill, a dropout ant,
A lone miniscule yippie of an ant!

Earlier that morning I sat on grass,
Thick lens in hand,
Searching his economic land;
I dug holes under a bank
And poked about, forked in my fingers,
So he must have stowed away on me.

But an ant ten miles at sea
Running without grass camouflage
And moving faster than the boat—
That was nothing if not something else!
A speck (cut-off fingernail size)
Scurried across the deck
With double-quick terror beneath an anchor line.

Ripe Banana Lands

Between temperate and tropic zones
Colors of spring and summer in fans
Of petals, unclenching, ripple out.
A rotten avocado falls at my feet.
An unsprayed sapodilla, moldy-holed,
Pocked and curled, dead to begin with,
Pricks out a dateless epitaph.
Hairy bulbs explode sapful
Of erzatz flowers, plastic eidolons.
Low waters never lapse, parched
Roots suck salty flumes, and one
Red-eyed hibiscus, the day's stub,
Smolders and ends with a sun
That flares in my ingenious eyes
Leveled to inspect time's losses.

Two's Company

Yesterday I spied a lizard screening our lunch,
Peeking in surreptitiously at our conversation.
But today, minding my own business in the sun,
Out of the corner of an eye I got an eyeful:
A lizardess (it must have been a lizardess) coyly
Clung to the wall beneath the bougainvillea,
While our vigorous, inquisitive friend boldly
Stood posed above her on the patio, preening,
Shimmying his tail, perking his tiny arrow head,
His whole body pleading. She turned her back—
He flicker-tongued a kind of saurian love-plea—
And then she shied herself voluptuously about,
Hopped to the floor and stretched out her consent . . .
But I slipped away so as not to spoil their lizardry.

Cockayne

A pair of bobbing plastic ducks,
True lovers, quacklessly floating,
Cradled and siamesed together
Across a swimming blue-eyed pool,
Drifted from side to length to side.
A soft, reluctant, inhaled wind
Rocked them through panoramas
Of Cockayne, vistas of Xanadu,
Immune to sandfly fleshly agonies.
Chameleons, members of the wedding,
Gaped as these featherless decoys
Swayed past in dream-locked ecstasy.
Bloating their wrinkled chests,
Frogs in a choir hopped up
And gulped and croaked with glee.
My own heart throbbed inside them,
My pale moon shone above them,
Enclosed them and enchanted them.

The Mutability of Flowers

Aloof and bodiless, swinging among rapturous chirps,
Emotional pulleys stretched and lifted me
Up to the topmost rainbows where they sat
Brooding, buds at a standstill, self-involved,
Or weaving their voices in choruses, or swooping
Below in flocks and somersaulting on the lawn.

But what is old today
Was foretold yesterday:
A twist in the wind's mystery,
An anguish that will pinch their faces,
Cloud-shivering in expectancy,
And drench and shrivel them
Under their faded rainbow shawls.

Only (O if only) I can keep them alive!
Sadness, new-mown, seeps into the earth,
Breathing its lustre on the memory.

All in a Bunch

Love's energy clings, twines
A lily's neck stretches over the wall
A violet pierces rock to grow
Among ruins
Fields of careless daisies
Leap-frog from meadow to meadow.

Pilgrimage

I

Remembering wild flowers in August
I went to mourn their autumn wounds.
Like an eye-witness at the scene,
I wandered stricken and speechless
Among dry reeds and cricket sounds.

II

Most flowers die in time
And dust as people do
Without a wind to push them.
Their petals turn the page
In colors, brown and crumble,
Then drop into the silence.

Mind's Miracle

Nothing but bare limbs, bare and at stake
In the knitting, cracking, breeding ground:
But birds like thoughts, thoughts like birds,
Converge from distant Springs before and after.

A Poem Windblown

How to depict a petal
   Stiffens my fingers,
   Withers my eyes.
But to describe the loss
   Even of one of my poorest poems:
It's like losing ten petals on both hands;
   Like a seagull dragging tarred wings on the beach;
   Like rebeing a bored, trapped child
Thrashing inside a father's arms
   On a rainy Sunday holiday sans joy.

Au Naturel

A poem without a thought
A poem spelled from feelings alone
Mentioning no name, not a word,
Yet deeply seen as if
Seen to an ocean's floor,
A poem self-wrung, self-skeined
From myriads of tiny nerve ends
Threaded through a careful eye.

Grand Canyon

Donkeying down to the Big Hole,
The banquet of memory, I crossed a world
Garbled with gigantic feelings, revivers
Of sandpit years, a backward-flickering eyetwist
Stuffing the tin pails, dredging the tunnels . . . .
And burst from time on foot, spun a round
Shadow, my cycloptic vision gaping
Among pathetic ruins, old photo-stained
Faces, dun-bronze and orange-red:
   Seven Sisters, meagred by erosion, wearing
      Prim sun-faded ruffs and stone-gray shawls;
         Wind-blown beehive cones, buzz-buzzing;
            Fields indexed in shelved realities, with not one
               Foot of grave in the Canyon's gusty bowels.
Assigning the spirit to preoccupation,
Freeing the petrified bird in the mind,
I splashed morning colors on the western sky,
Stepped into my long-abandoned landscapes,
Palm-cupped and drank a hand-made lake
Of swallows in one gulp of promises.

The Source

Thousand-tongued
    Haranguing lava rock and cliff in frothing masses
      Orgasmic argosies freighted with tidal sperm
       Tilted horizons crashing upon their knees
Embracing whiteness with spume-light fingers
    Then churned in whirlpools of oblivion
      Sucked up and parched and marrow-drained
Where claws and spines, scales, coral, shipwrecks
    And fluted bones, shells and castaway cans
Leak ink from a poet's pen
    Upon a scrolled and wordless beach.

Glimpse

From the cliff I see
Low-tide boulders, undressed rocks
Stark in their lewdness,

Wave-splashed, wind-streaked,
With weeds and molluscs
Clamped to their backs.

Fall

A leaf fell down on my thoughts
From that inner forest of silence;
But my grasp was not large enough
To count all the things it veined,
And let it slip through my mind.

Caterpillar

Clumsy, grubby insect
With no nip or needle,
No ant stubbornness
Or spidery guile:
O future butterfly,
My eyes search the road
So as not to squish you—
For the sake of wings
Crawl where you will.

Variations on a Spider

I

Spider in the head
  Spider under the roof of the ego
    Spider behind the skins of my windows
Your six pairs of shadow pursue each gleam
  Through labyrinthine intimacies
    Down into dooms too deep for thought.

II

Pirouetting tight-rope dancer twirling
  On spectre-thin strands of umbilical moon-dew,
    Merging instinct with grasp, thought with act,
Obedient to his own tumultuous harmonies,
  He dangles and sways, clings and surveys
    A self-spun self, glaring through savage prisms.

III

Spiders sleep a curious sleep
  With three rows of shut-eye, three of open
    (Some have twice three, blinking, open and shut)
But always in touch, always within hearshot,
  Their executionary legs and pincers
    Tucked into innocent slits of mouths.

IV

Spellbound and crucifixed, splayed upon Orphic strings,
    These mummy-cocoons, moods of a momentary life
(Their newborn cries tuned to their death rattles)
    Dwindle and sag, billowing in time's weather:
Fog-dust tender moths' wings plucked and gallowed;
    Nagging clockwork crickets' riddles unriddled;
Windblown fireflies' elves-eye candles quenched;
    Sun-spun figment-of-fancy butterflies fact-bound.

Knock-Knock

Vague horrors freeze the spines of flies
Who come into the parlor. *Who's there?*
A hoo-doo voodoo strangler, that's who;
Or an old beggar woman with a witch's cackle
Knitting a shroud; or maybe a squatting
Yogi, crossed heart and navel, meditating murder;
Or maybe a dancing Shiva twitching its feasted legs;
Or maybe a fist walking toward him on its fingers;
Or maybe nothing, nothing but the shadow
Of his own fear congealed into a hunched fang.

Another Chance

Sky-conceived snowflake
Heaven-hewed six-sided newborn twirler
Spun by the myriad out of the blue
To fall upon bare trees, bowed heads and barren lives
Congealing and glazing refuse and failure
Rapping on eyesight with feathery touch
To open up, to fill their bowls, to see again
Fiestas in the clouds
Washing the air with gala white,
Constellations of beauty unwrinkling the ground.

Adam to Eve

Before we were ours
I dared to wonder:
How would I kiss your
Mouths, name your toes,
Fall from your clouds
Upon your breasts,
Explore you, open you,
Deepen slowly into you,
Then subside within you.

Beginning

Dusk or dawn twilight,
Moist, open, tight:
Where am I in you?
The lens of insight
Blurs and grows dim:
What is that blaze?
Moving with your moves,
Sinking yet rising:
Let me go! Keep me in!
Until the twilight
Deepens to quiet.

Root

Stripped leaves leave the artichoke's heart
    Unprepared for nakedness;
But in the shadowy pleasures of her sweet
    Exfoliations, grown out of earth,
        Alive for me while I'm alive,
I nibble at her fronds to reach the core
    Buried deep down near birth.

Scenario of a Scene

I

At the Party

After the quake of your going from me
   My cheekbones cracked a smile
      Pride wallpapered a massive tic
And I felt each voice in the room
   Merge into seethings of whisper
      Guilt-stained with our betrayal.
Unpoised, a crevasse at my side,
I toppled into your absence.

II

Phantom

At home with a stranger sipping my wine,
Without love, without lust, without lies
Of pleasure, I caught sight of my own
Face to face on the sheen of a window,
Miraged and framed, a graven myth,
Myself from without without you.

Blind Date

As I got up, surrounded by things,
A Swedish modern chest grew breasts—
The shadowy globes of her absence;
Plucked from a snarl of roots and wires,
A lamp bloomed on the floor and shocked;
A mop became a language of strings
And rinsed the steppingstones of words;
A toadstool hassock on the rug
Tripped me to say the lies of love,
The usual decorous useless bric-a-bric
Broken in breathing as the door shut.

Man-Eater

Suspicious fish
Groping in a downed sea of my losses,
Poking into the asthmatic darkness,
I shimmied to the sparkle of her lure.
At the first twitch, the hook of a finger,
Hoodwinked, I bit,
Her scorn jammed down my heart,
My feelings taut and jerking
Miles away from the rocking boat.

Resemblances

When sleep dims out
The faint remains of day
And the mind's arrow,
Sight of uncertainty,
Shoots behind the arras,
I eavesdrop on myself
Bickering with a stranger
Inside a loveless dream.

Confessional

Those inside weepings, weepings,
Whispers and apparitions were clothed
In a strangeness that darkened my mind.

I learned to speak your name without a sound,
Afraid of hope, playing a child's game
Self-locked in the closet of my pride.

The Gift

Pride-pain of giving in,
Giving up, shorn of vanity,
Bearing the gift of hair
For witch-blonde false Delilah!
Turning the knob of submission,
I enter the menace of forgiveness.
Who forgives whom? And for what?
A door slams shut in my mind.

Aftermath

A momentary sunset
Across my inner lids
Closed the day for me,
Shuttered the useless
Word-weary wisdom
Pulsing inside my head,
Rammed my trudging legs
To climb a beard
Of arguments to bed.

In a tangle of limbs
Under one blanket,
Cold inside out,
Our souls wrangle
And squirm far apart.

Losses

I

For Henry Rago

Time hurries us, hurries us, hurries us
Fumbling, stalling, to mete our punishments.
We tape-measure our wholecloth aspirations,
We stroke, we calm our sensualities,
We pay lip-service to annual mortality.

Sighs, heaven-stories high,
Usher in this good man's holiday,
Evoke his intimate recollection,
Echo the priestly eulogies,
Angered, panicked by the loss
Of all his hearts, his ripe
And human melons starved by years,
Hungry for him in an empty orchard.

There are degrees of death. Shut in and sealed
Under the eyelid and lip of immortality,
We lose sight of him, sound of him
At the petrified instant of finality,
The nails of grief stricken into the wood.

Faith's paradox, reasonable superstition,
Bridges bewilderment and separation.

II

Recalling Oscar

I stood at sand's edge
Clicking old sounds
My automatic mind revolved,
Revisited the boulder-field
Cliffs, replayed their organ shapes,
Fantasized their requiem:
Bach's moods of the sea.
I reached for sight
Of his old image at my side,
Remembering laughter shouts.
Our flat stones skimmed the scalloped waves
As we twirled happily;
Our fingers dug purple sand
(Gold specks glistening from our nails)
And then he fell racing up the weedy hillside.

III

For Dr. Leonard P. Wershub

1

There is a desert under the grass
Where he lies. He has been called back,
Cannot call back, will never call back—
The umbilical switchboard is buzzing.
He who made no joke of life, whose poise
Sustained a keen and operating will,
A blade of light beneath the polar dome
Where death's malignancy was quarantined,
Has tripped and fallen from the ladderless
Years down sixty-seven echoing rungs
Into an armchair, stunned, heart-stopped.

2

As though she had fathomed alone
The quicksand of his departure
We gaze spellbound at his widow
Grasping at ungraspable limits.

We measure her dignity by her dry
Eyes that shall never meet his again.
Love has become her looking-glass,
A mirror to the invisible.

Reunion

When I dusted Grandma's portrait
Memories sneezed in my mind—
A card game of hearts
Outlasting half a century.

She mended my mother's scolds
Cut her apron strings
Tucked away lullabies
Played pranks and finger-
Shadows on the bedroom wall.

On the cracked starched canvas
Grandma's wrinkled bosom
Heaved in reunion:
Out of a gilt frame
In restless storage
She beamed back at me.

Aspects of Papa

I

The Question

I saw my father in the wintry shadow
The day we crossed fields on horseback.
On that perfect neutral ground, match-
Maker of mood between father and son,
We sought for speech among wooded shapes,
Found a twig begging to be seen, noticed
The golden willingness of autumn leaves.
My legs stretched tension into the stirrups.
We studied dumb ground. The silence gripped,

Reined in my crucial question
Until a bird's flutter mixed
With the echo of a hunter's shot.

II

The Failing Bell

This was the first time I flew over his grave.
It was then that I knew he was there—
Among tombstone dots—my father
Whose toil and love did father me,
Who shackled his young promises
To dying years of fatherhood.

His hands unfolded bolts of cloth
Not for a shroud but for the doctor's fee
While I lay quarantined, choked in my room,
And never heard him tiptoe to the door
Eavesdropping for each rasp of breath.

As I flew above childhood through autumn clouds
My father was everywhere in still language.
I felt his anger-prod of perfection
But could not hear the failing bell,
And soon the grave became a speck
Among trees rusting in orange age.

III

Reflections

Accumulating the faces of my father
On my own, fluttering through time
Like pictures in a gallery corridor
(As though all fathers looked alike,
Myself my father, my own son myself)
The mind recounts counter-clockwise.

Sharing one name, eating common bread,
Our identity flourished in a hoard
Of unshed images, remains of shadows,
And I still hear, evoked and metronomed,
My brother's violin, my sister's piano,
My mute poetic Roland's horn.

Hello & Goodbye

I

Going on living,
Disremembering the pain of friends who are dead,
Was at first a ceaseless
Gnawing and twisting worm in the heart.

Old habit could pluck
Their telephone voices fresh in my mind—
Then suddenly, one day
I dialed to an electronic absence.

II

At their wrenched departure
My self-pity was as large as my sorrow;
Their remains were scarecrow
Clothes hung somewhere in death's field.

Meanwhile, as always, I exist,
Honor the rites, pour out the wine,
Raising my spirit with theirs—
I never leave them out of the new noise.

For My Grandson
(Blake Nelson Sobiloff)

Beginning a lifetime,
A sleep-awakened time,
Your time for the common world—
Our customary miracle—
You clasp a finger of light.

Mirages of excitement
Skimmer in your eyes
Sun-beamed by the dazzle
Of a dancing prism:
Father's kaleidoscope
Twinkling over your crib.

Hushed in your mother's cuddle,
Tranquil to her whispers,
Your new mind adds pieces
Of people, conversations,
You bubble early round sounds
With a burp for her approval.

While you crawl and stare
Through the crib shutters,
Grandpa's milieu dwindles—
A change in his mealtime too
Triggers temperamental tantrums.
So long! He has to go now,
Flying away with his white hair.

Hitchhiker

Barefoot, dirty, drenched in a sweatshirt,
I jiggled and waited, hoped and whistled,
Picked wild bouquets of prickly thistle,
Turned down both thumbs at hooting cars,
Troubled deaf heaven with deaf-mute signs
And summoned every plea and ploy, looking
Before and after, hopscotching on hot macadam,
Until some tooting salesman from Samaria
Picked me up on my way out to this far.

Arizona Nightmare

Coyotes rushing to rejoin their mates
Howling inside me keep the night awake.
Faithful to their shadows, on the sky,
They split through chaos in twilit packs,
Huddle together in barren regions,
Sip dry water, suck cactus sap,
Swallow hot-veined flowers that bloom
Through cracks of diamond rocks.
Bellies down, close to the city line,
They spring into my solitude.

Way Back Then

Where do I begin? 42 years of sleep ago
On the Arizona desert, a midget of 14,
Barracked together with sixteen other kids
In low steel cots where no secret was covered,
Nightmared by "Mama!" screams. I pull time's arm—
All of their lost, new-minted faces gush
Through time's slots and chutes, pocketfuls
Of lives long since replaced by other lives,
Deaths, traumas, dramas and amours . . . .

My mind
Winks and recounts those fun-weird years
When kissing began, when I stood
Up under the Chi Omega porch
Baying for Juliet: *Hist, she appears,*
She primps, leaning her sun-globe fronts
From the lucky balcony window!
My Jack in the Beanstalk grows, my arms
Stretch out within a fingertip of touch . . . .

Then I'd slip
Once more into the taut white iron slot
Upon the half-asleep porch to finish
Love-making in the head. The anvil chorus
Of conscience began: Old testamental fingers wagged:
"It's not nice! What will become?
You deserve to be too young to love!" And so I dripped

Back to myself, back then, back to Jack
Squirming and stuttering, George cachinnating,
Paul pleading with demons to wake up . . . .

And the rest of the sixteen—a bagful
Of aggies bunched for a 7:40 class
Until the dawn's too early light
Staggers a row of clocks, groans, hails,
Bells and gongs that shake the beds.

Sheep in Wolf's Clothing

His frenzy turned off
Dr. Jekyl returns and combs his hair
Assays his eyes vexed on the rack
And begs himself for mercy ("O *forgive*
Me my deceit!") the self-distracted
Judas Janus of his own pardon.

To earn or borrow someone else's sorrow
His immortal/mortal guise
Repents and squelches all defaulted promises
In unnatural/natural depths
Of lunar cravings, stroking, lulling lunar cravings.
Wailing with laughter, he overthrows
His children, child by child,
Looms in a mirrored trance
And werewolf leaps at innocence . . . .
Then mourns his moods:

"I the father, lover, husband—
I, I, I—
At the sick height of my career
A fever-stricken plague carrier,
Infector of my selves unquarantined:
Who am I? Where am I? Why am I?
Torn-to-pieces past offenses
Lie in protective sleep custody,

Refuged in a merciful cave,
Until past midnight when the dance
Of argument and counter-argument begins.
My mind is its own enemy
And tears apart the torso of my crime."

The Feathered Tarbaby

I

The public is stripped of sight, stuffed
With shouts, drenched with its own rain,
Wearing a hate lid, stepping a goose-step
In and out of sleep (perchance to dream)
Clucking and pecking in the chicken run
Beak by bigger beak, weak by not so weak,
All plucked on the rails to Babel and Baal.

The revel of the ages—a feathered tarbaby's
Public body linked with neck-chain exile!
Stifling the voices of love singers,
They howl, outhowling the wail of Galilee,
Horrorizing old and new thoughts, waving
Official tickets to God-om, spilling
Someone else's blood, laying dead feats
And spent facts at freedom's foundation—
Magic sex-palpitating flutters of silent
Kisses strewn across carcasses of flies . . . .

II

I gaze across History's concourse
At unknown kids, blotched and dimmed,
Splashed across a hurrying conscience;
Then look at the time's new classroom faces
Puffing the wars away, tripping up disappearing ladders,

Still full of misspellings, Sunday-school crayon-ripe
"Thou Shalt Nots" on their killerless minds,
Accused of crimes of joy, yet not too young
For death's depravities or life's banalities.

Buck-passing elders, the fumblers of these young,
With clotted eyelids, hearts sered on both sides,
Live out their bags of bones, seventy or more
Times outsmarted by our enemy—*Whose
Enemy?*—whose enemy becomes our enemy.

In a Polynesian Restaurant

Whose haunts are these
Where tongues stick out
Of masks on walls
Like blood-tipped spears?
Tall mirrors reflect
Conch shells, whales' teeth,
Bony-needled urchins;
Also, a king's canoe
And a mummied skull
With straw for hair,
Beads for eyes
Hung from a pole—
Totems, trophies
Of lost or won
Forgotten wars.

What spells are cast?
What dice of bones?

Delphic

Darkness surrounds the question
I ask my drowsy owl:
In which old year did laughter die?

I listen to a forest clock of crickets,
Watch opposite windows between branches
Divide and redouble the moon.

My blinking owl
My bleak austerity
Hoots across the silence.

Let Me Tell You How I Feel

My twilight eye sinks
   My head minds a circumstance
      My ears in whorls swallow up words:
The steps where I have been hound where I am
   A key turns in the latched quandary
      The room light, deep in thought, widens:
A standstill, tall and listening, throws
   A flat shadow through the eye-slat:
My sunless dawn, without a rooster's crow,
   Twists over to the other side of night.

Surprise

I climbed my limbs into wings.
One shallow wing fell down
And down I fell. What could I think
Up in the sky? What does a bird

Think? Weird, crippled sky-flier!
Bird-man with one gimpy wing!
The earth, falling, amazes me
As I rise to meet the ground.